D0995279

YORK NOTES
KEY STAGE 3

Twelfth Night

William Shakespeare

Note by David Pinnington

 Longman

York Press

York Press
322 Old Brompton Road, London SW5 9JH

Pearson Education Limited
Edinburgh Gate, Harlow, Essex CM20 2JE, United Kingdom
Associated companies, branches and representatives throughout
the world

© Librairie du Liban *Publishers* and Pearson Education Limited 2000

All rights reserved. No part of this publication may be reproduced, stored in a
retrieval system, or transmitted in any form or by any means, electronic,
mechanical, photocopying, recording or otherwise, without either the prior
written permission of the Publishers or a licence permitting restricted copying
in the United Kingdom issued by the Copyright Licensing Agency Ltd,
90 Tottenham Court Road, London W1P 0LP.

First published 2000
Revised 2001
ISBN 0-582-43145-X

Illustrated by Tony Chance
Designed by Vicki Pacey
Phototypeset by Gem Graphics, Trenance, Mawgan Porth, Cornwall
Produced by Pearson Education China Limited, Hong Kong

Contents

Preface

Health Warning: This study guide will help you to understand the play, but should not replace the reading of the original text and/or study in class.

York Notes Key Stage 3 guides are designed to give you the help you need to tackle the plays of Shakespeare, a requirement for the National Tests.

The English tests (sometimes called SATs) are taken in the final term of Year 9. Pupils must sit two papers: Paper 1 on Reading and Writing and Paper 2 on Key Scenes taken from a Shakespeare play chosen by your teacher. The papers are marked by external examiners and the results are published at the end of July, in the form of a Level for English.

This symbol shows the Key Scenes which form the core of the play

Each of these Notes will provide a biography of Shakespeare and close examination of one of the set plays, and include a summary of each scene in the play as well as detailed summaries of the Key Scenes on which the National Test focuses. To check your progress, tests are included on each Act. Commentary is also provided on themes, characters and language.

York Notes Key Stage 3 are written by English teachers and examiners with an expert knowledge of the subject. They show you how to succeed in your Key Stage 3 tests, taking you through the play and offering practical guidance.

York Notes Key Stage 3 guides are ideal for
* Understanding Shakespeare
* Preparing for exams
* Improving your Level

The author of this Note is David Pinnington. He currently teaches in Devon and is a Senior Examiner in English and English Literature for a major GCSE examination board.

The text used in this Notes is the Arden Shakespeare Series, Routledge, 1975.

Introduction

How to study a Shakespeare play

The National Curriculum in English makes it compulsory for Key Stage 3 students to study for an examination on a Shakespeare play. This book aims to guide you through this task by explaining carefully the development of the story of your chosen play, and by setting out the important features which you will need to include in your examination response.

Shakespeare wrote his plays for performance on a stage. The best way in to this play is of course to go to a theatre and see it live. If you are unable to do this, then hire it on a video or listen to it on audiotape or CD.

One of the chief reasons for the greatness of these plays is that they are entertaining. They are studied in class because their true quality may not be revealed in a single visit to the theatre.

Use the points given below as a check-list to help you to a fuller understanding of what the play is about:

∗ Follow the story-line – who are the winners and losers? Does the story end in the way you would have chosen? Or would you change its ending? Why?

∗ Look at the characters – which ones do you like and which ones do you dislike? Are you happy with what happens to them at the end of the play?

∗ Look at the staging of the play – is the set what you would have expected? If not, why not? Do you think that you might have been mistaken in your view of what the set should have been? Why?

∗ Look at the costumes – are they what you would have expected? Again, if not, why not? Do the characters' costumes tell you anything about the characters themselves?

✳ Think of the special effects, like lighting and sound –
what did they add to your enjoyment of the production?

Remember each generation interprets Shakespeare in a
way that makes sense to its audiences. If you see
Shakespeare's plays as museum pieces, you are unlikely
to be very entertained by them.

Think about this: the best students are those who
identify with the plays they watch. What do you think
this play can tell you about life in the new millennium?

Find answers to that question and you will truly
have made a success of your first experience with
Shakespeare study.

Shakespeare's life

Family life

William Shakespeare was born at Stratford-upon-Avon in 1564. There is a record of his christening on 26 April, so we can assume he was born shortly before that date. His father, John Shakespeare, was a glove-maker and trader who later became high bailiff of Stratford; his mother, Mary Arden, was the daughter of a landowner.

In 1582 Shakespeare married Anne Hathaway, a woman eight years older than himself. Their first child, Susanna, was christened in May 1583, and in 1585 twins Hamnet and Judith were born.

Shakespeare lived during the reign of Queen Elizabeth I, a period known as the Elizabethan Age.

Writing

Sometime after 1585 Shakespeare left Stratford and went to London where he became an actor and a dramatist. He worked first with a group of actors called Lord Pembroke's Men and later with a company called the Lord Chamberlain's Men (later the King's Men). His earliest plays were performed around 1590 to 1594. He was successful in the theatre from the start.

In 1601 Shakespeare wrote the comedy *Twelfth Night*.

The last years

Although Shakespeare lived and worked for most of his life in London, he obviously did not forget Stratford, and in about 1610 he returned to live there permanently.

Shakespeare wrote a will in January 1616, leaving money to people he knew in Stratford and to some of his actor-friends. He died on 23 April 1616.

Background to the play

The feast of 'Twelfth Night'

'Twelfth Night' was the name given to the last day of the Elizabethan Christmas festivities, which were celebrated enthusiastically throughout the land. In the Christian calendar Twelfth Night is known as the Feast of Epiphany. It commemorates the coming of the Magi, sometimes known as the Three Kings, to the stable in Bethlehem with their gifts of gold, frankincense and myrrh.

Shakespeare's title to his play, however, has nothing to do with its story – it refers to when it was performed, probably on 6 January 1602. It is likely that the alternative title, *What You Will*, also refers to the festive associations, a signal to the audience that the play is an entertainment for a special occasion.

The plot

The plot of *Twelfth Night* probably comes from two sources: a short story in English called *The Historie of Apolonius and Silla* and an Italian play, *Gl'Ingannati* (The Deceived Ones).

Most **romantic comedies** (see Literary Terms) in Elizabethan times included certain types of characters, known as **stock characters** (see Literary Terms) such as: a cunning servant; a pedant or hypocrite; a pair of young lovers; and twins.

Confusions of identity were a common feature of Elizabethan plays, as was disguise, and particularly men disguised as women, or women disguised as men.

Because these elements were so common, Shakespeare's audience must have come into the theatre expecting to see certain things.

Malvolio and Puritanism

Twelfth Night was sometimes given the title *Malvolio* when it was performed in Shakespeare's day. This is because Shakespeare had turned a character 'type' into a memorable individual. The Elizabethan audience was interested in the depiction of Malvolio as a Puritan. The Puritans were a religious group who had condemned theatres and other entertainments because they thought they corrupted people. They thought plays contained too much sex and violence, and were unchristian and the cause of sin. Puritans dressed plainly, disliked drinking, and had strict ideas about how people should behave. Malvolio thus has all the characteristics which the pleasure-seeking Elizabethan audience hated. There is no obvious sympathy for him in the play whatsoever. However, Malvolio's final threat of revenge is ominous – in fact, the Puritans succeeded in closing down the theatres in 1642.

Think of a modern-day Malvolio who tries to impose their moral standards on everybody else

The stage

The stage used in the Elizabethan theatre was very simple. The setting of each scene was created by a combination of words and music. For example, when the sea captain tells Viola that 'This is Illyria, lady.' (I.2.2) the audience would have to imagine the country of Illyria. To an Elizabethan audience the name Illyria would conjure up an almost magical region, far away from the real world, where all the improbabilities of the story could be accepted.

Illustrated summary

Viola: shipwrecked on the coast of Illyria.

The Duke Orsino meets Viola who is now dressed as a man – Cesario. She falls in love with him.

Sebastian, Viola's brother is brought ashore on another part of the coast.

Maria, Aguecheek and Sir Toby, plot to make a fool of Malvolio.

Malvolio

Duke Orsino is in love with Olivia. However, Olivia falls in love with Cesario (Viola).

All is revealed and Olivia marries Sebastian – The count marries Viola.

Summaries

Act I

Scene 1

Orsino loves
Olivia

Orsino, Duke of Illyria, sits in his palace listening to music. He thinks about the many emotions that music inspires in people who are in love. The duke himself is in love with Olivia and his mood is sentimental. He soon becomes tired of the music and stops the musicians. He speaks of the 'spirit of love', its excessive needs and its fickleness.

Orsino's page, Curio, tries to distract him and asks if he would like to go hunting. The duke replies that he is already hunting the 'noblest' prey – Olivia. He is waiting for a reply to a message he has sent to her. When Valentine, the messenger, enters he has some disappointing news. Olivia's brother has died and she has vowed to mourn his death for seven years, during which time no one will see her face. Orsino is not put off by this: if Olivia 'hath a heart of that fine frame' (line 33) to mourn a brother, then she would be even more sensitive and loyal to him as a lover.

Comment

The setting of the play is important. Shakespeare's comedies are set in distant places because audiences find these more romantic. Also, the softly sentimental music matches Orsino's very musical language, emphasising the theme of romance.

We learn about Orsino's attitude to love in this scene: he is as much in love with Olivia as he is with the idea of love itself.

Notice the **simile** (see Literary Terms) comparing the sea to the 'spirit of love' which is never satisfied. At the end of the play Orsino will quickly change his affections from Olivia to Viola (V.1.265–6).

Scene 2

Viola is
shipwrecked

On the coast of Illyria, Viola, a sea captain and some sailors have recently survived a shipwreck. The captain tells Viola that he saw her twin brother, Sebastian, tying himself to a mast just before the boat was split in two. The captain watched Sebastian being swept away by the waves and thinks that, although it is possible he survived, it is more likely that they are the only survivors.

For giving her some small hope that her brother might be alive, Viola gives the captain some gold. She asks him if he is familiar with the country they have landed in. He is, and says he was born and brought up 'Not three hours' travel from this place' (line 23). Viola learns that Illyria is ruled by the 'noble' Duke Orsino. She remembers her father mentioning him in the past – the duke was a bachelor in those days and according to the captain still is. However, when the captain visited Illyria recently, he heard that Orsino was seeking the love of the 'fair' Olivia. Viola asks about Olivia and the captain tells her that she is a 'virtuous maid' (a virgin) whose father died a year ago leaving her under the protection of a brother, who has also just died. Since then she has turned her back on the world.

Viola decides
to disguise
herself

Viola wishes she could serve Olivia, perhaps because she herself is also brotherless. The captain tells her that would be impossible because Olivia will see no one. Viola devises a plan. She will serve the duke instead. She promises to pay the captain if he will help her disguise herself as a eunuch (castrated man) and then take her to Orsino. She can sing, and she plays many musical instruments; in this way she will make the duke employ her. The captain agrees to help her.

Comment   Notice the similarities and the differences between Viola
and what we have learned about Olivia at this point.
They are both brotherless, both recently orphaned. Their
names make an almost exact anagram. Yet Olivia can
express her grief publicly and Viola cannot – she has to
work out a way to survive.

Viola's disguise begins a complicated series of
concealments and confusions which continues
throughout the play.

There is a reference to music in relation to the duke and
Viola, perhaps suggesting that she and Orsino might
eventually fall in love.

Scene 3   The scene shifts to Olivia's house where her uncle, Sir

Toby Belch, is complaining about the way his niece is
mourning her brother's death. He thinks she is
overreacting. Maria, Olivia's servant, tells him that Olivia
disapproves of his late nights, his clothes and his

We meet **Sir Toby ...**	drinking bouts. She has also complained of the 'foolish knight' that Sir Toby has brought home to woo her. Sir Andrew Aguecheek is a stupid waster, says Maria, but Sir Toby disagrees. Not only is Sir Andrew rich, he replies, but he can play the viola-di-gamba and speak three or four languages. Maria replies that Sir Andrew is a fool, a quarreller, a coward and a drunkard. And just as Sir Toby is making the extravagant claim that all their drinking amounts to is a few toasts to Olivia, Sir Andrew appears.
... and Sir **Andrew**	Sir Toby introduces the knight to Maria, who proceeds to make him look every bit as stupid as she has claimed. After she has gone Sir Toby discovers that his friend is feeling very pessimistic about his chances with Olivia and is planning to ride home the next day. She will see no one, he says, and even if she did, she certainly would not want to have anything to do with him. Besides, adds Sir Andrew, the Count Orsino is wooing her. Sir Toby manages to persuade Aguecheek to stay for another month by telling him that he has heard Olivia say she would never marry an older, more intelligent and more important person than herself. Sir Toby makes Sir Andrew admit that he is a good dancer. They will have a lot of fun if he stays and shows off his steps. The two knights agree to continue their 'revels'.

Comment   A new set of characters is introduced and the play moves from a romantic world down to a more earthy, fun-loving one. Sir Toby's explosive first line reveals his relationship to Olivia and the kind of character he is – a man devoted to pleasure.

Note the way Maria handles Sir Toby and Sir Andrew. She is clever with words and her frank opinions of them suggest the important role she will play in the comic **sub-plot** (see Literary Terms) which is to follow.

The relationship of Sir Toby to Sir Andrew is clear here: Sir Toby makes a fool of his 'friend'. The 'three thousand ducats a year' (line 22) are significant in their relationship because Sir Andrew pays for Sir Toby's pleasures and must be kept happy.

Olivia has now two men after her: Duke Orsino and the ridiculous Sir Andrew Aguecheek, and Malvolio will later make a third. The comic sub-plot reflects the main plot in which the duke pursues Olivia.

Scene 4

Duke Orsino sends 'Cesario' to tell Olivia of his love

Viola, disguised as Cesario, has become a great favourite with the Duke Orsino, even though he has known 'him' for only three days. Taking Cesario aside, Orsino commands him to carry love messages to Olivia. He urges the youth to be persistent, even to the point of being rude, until Olivia agrees to receive him. Cesario must tell Olivia of Orsino's passion and his sorrow. The duke believes that because Cesario is so young and handsome – sounding and looking almost like a young girl himself – Olivia is more likely to respond favourably. Cesario will be rewarded well if he is successful. In a revealing aside Cesario (Viola) complains that she will be wooing on behalf of a man whom she herself would like to marry.

Scene 5

KEY SCENE

In Olivia's house Maria is telling Feste, the clown, that Olivia is annoyed by his absence. She wants to know where he has been and jokes that Olivia will hang him for playing truant. Feste does not care. 'Many a good hanging prevents a bad marriage' (line 19), he says. Maria advises him to prepare a good excuse because Olivia is about to appear. When Olivia enters, accompanied by her steward, Malvolio, she is very solemn and in no mood to listen to the clown. She orders him away, but Feste eventually amuses her and she softens towards him. Malvolio, however, finds the clown's joking rude and not at all funny. He wonders why Olivia finds such pleasure in someone so feeble in mind and body. Olivia responds by telling Malvolio off for his pride and intolerance. There is no offence in Feste's joking, she says, because he is an 'allowed fool', permitted to make harmless jests.

A handsome 'gentleman' wants to see Olivia

Maria announces that a handsome young gentleman has arrived who wishes to speak with Olivia, but he is being delayed at the gate by Sir Toby Belch. Olivia instructs Maria to fetch her uncle, since he will be talking rubbish, and Malvolio is told to make some excuse for Olivia if the visitor is from the Duke Orsino. While Maria and Malvolio are gone Sir Toby enters, and his niece tries to find out who the 'gentleman' is. But her uncle is too drunk to make sense; when he has stumbled off Olivia sends Feste to look after him.

Malvolio returns and informs Olivia that the young man insists on speaking to her. He will accept no excuses. Olivia asks what sort of man he is and is told that he is young and handsome, with a sharp voice. Olivia agrees to see him but only in the presence of Maria, who is instructed to veil Olivia's face.

When Cesario (Viola) enters he starts to pay her compliments, while cleverly avoiding Olivia's questions about himself. It is clear that Olivia is very interested in this handsome young man, but he will not tell her his message while other people are present. Olivia sends Maria and the attendants away. Cesario tells Olivia that

'Cesario' tells Olivia how much Duke Orsino loves her	his message comes from Orsino's heart and he asks to be allowed to see her face. When she unveils herself Cesario is full of admiration, and is sorry that the owner of such beauty should be so cruel as to never have children and thus 'leave the world no copy' (line 246). Don't worry, replies Olivia, I will leave an account of my beauty in writing when I die; every respect of it will be written down and 'copied'.
Olivia says she cannot love Duke Orsino	In spite of Cesario's declaration that Orsino truly loves her, Olivia says she cannot love him in return, despite all his virtues. He must not continue to woo her. Yet if Cesario would like to return, Olivia will be happy to see him. She tries to pay him, but Cesario proudly declines to accept the gold she offers, and leaves.
Olivia sends Malvolio to speak to 'Cesario'	By now completely infatuated with Cesario, Olivia calls Malvolio and tells him to follow the messenger with a ring which she claims he has left behind. She asks Malvolio to tell Cesario that if he returns again tomorrow she will provide more reasons why she cannot love the duke. By the end of the scene Olivia has fallen in love with Cesario, the duke's messenger. The ring is a trick to make him return.

Comment	Feste's attempt to prove that Olivia is a fool (lines 55–70) by mocking her state of mourning gives us clues about how she will behave later in the scene. Olivia describes Malvolio's character (lines 89–93) in words which are meant to stick in our minds. He is shown as an enemy of pleasure and wit who takes himself and everybody else too seriously. This prepares the audience for the trick that will be played on him later in the play.

Y

Olivia is clearly intelligent – she appreciates the **puns** (see Literary Terms) of the clown and her characterisation of Malvolio is very accurate. However, we also find out that she does not always do what she believes she will do – she quickly forgets her vows to mourn her brother and see no one, and allows herself to become attracted to Cesario.

The conversation between Olivia and Cesario starts off in **prose** and moves to the poetic form of **blank verse** (see Literary Terms) to emphasise the discussion of love.

When Cesario tells Olivia that Orsino loves her 'with adoration, fertile tears, / With groans that thunder love, with sighs of fire' (lines 259–60) he is using exaggerated language known as **hyperbole** (see Literary Terms) which is common in love poetry.

In spite of all his qualities, Olivia cannot love Orsino (lines 261–6), yet she is amazed at how quickly she has fallen for Cesario (line 299). The irrational nature of love is a major theme of the play.

At the end of Act I Orsino loves Olivia who loves Cesario (Viola) who secretly loves Orsino. This love triangle is the key to the plot and its resolution. It creates a basic **dramatic irony** (see Literary Terms) in which the audience knows more than the characters.

Test (Act I)

Fill in the blanks

Duke Orsino lives in .... and is in love with ...., who has vowed to mourn her brother's death for .... years.

Meanwhile, two identical twins, ... and ...., have been shipwrecked off the coast of Illyria and have become separated. Viola decides to dress as a .... and call herself .... so that she can serve the duke in his court.

Sir .... does not approve of his niece's decision to go into mourning because he wants his friend, Sir .... to woo and marry her. When .... is employed by .... to take messages to .... she begins to fall in love with him. To complicate things further, ... becomes attracted to .... and tries to get 'him' to return.

By the end of Act I, ... loves Olivia, who loves ...., who is really ...., who secretly loves ....

Give modern words for these words used by Shakespeare

1 validity (I.1.12)	6 murmur (I.2.32)
2 pitch (I.1.12)	7 allow (I.2.59)
3 element (I.1.26)	8 wit (I.2.61)
4 cloistress (I.1.28)	9 substractors (I.3.34)
5 Elysium (I.2.4)	10 Lenten (I.5.9)

C | Quiz

1 Who does Orsino love

2 Who is Olivia in mourning for?

3 Who helps Viola when she is shipwrecked?

4 What is the name of Olivia's female servant?

5 What is the name of Viola's brother

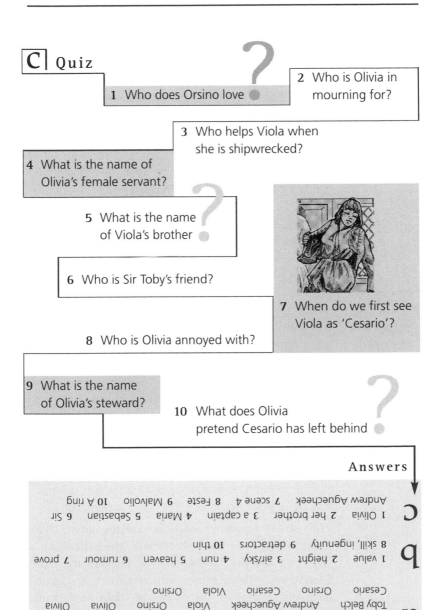

6 Who is Sir Toby's friend?

7 When do we first see Viola as 'Cesario'?

8 Who is Olivia annoyed with?

9 What is the name of Olivia's steward?

10 What does Olivia pretend Cesario has left behind

Answers

C 1 Olivia 2 her brother 3 a captain 4 Maria 5 Sebastian 6 Sir Andrew Aguecheek 7 scene 4 8 Feste 9 Malvolio 10 A ring

b 1 value 2 height 3 airy/sky 4 nun 5 heaven 6 rumour 7 prove 8 skill, ingenuity 9 detractors 10 thin

a Illyria Olivia seven Viola Sebastian eunuch Cesario
Toby Belch Andrew Aguecheek Viola Orsino Olivia Olivia
Cesario Orsino Cesario Viola Orsino
Cesario

Act II

Scene 1

Sebastian is shipwrecked

On the coast of Illyria we discover that Viola's twin brother, Sebastian, has not drowned after all. He was rescued from the sea by Antonio, another sea captain, who has been looking after him. Sebastian is very unhappy; he is convinced that Viola has drowned in the shipwreck.

Antonio is keen to help him but Sebastian wants to be alone with his grief. Yet Sebastian trusts Antonio and tells him something about himself and his background, in particular his beautiful twin sister who resembled him so much. Antonio asks if he could be his servant.

Sebastian goes to Duke Orsino's court

Sebastian says no: he does not want to be a burden to Antonio any longer. He tells him he is going to Orsino's court and says goodbye.

Although Antonio has many dangerous enemies in Orsino's court, he decides to follow him there.

Scene 2

Malvolio talks to 'Cesario'

Cesario (Viola) is followed by Malvolio who asks him if he is the same person who was recently with the Countess Olivia. Cesario replies that he is, and Malvolio holds out the ring which he has been told to return to the youth. Malvolio tells him sarcastically that he would have been spared the trouble of returning it to Cesario if Cesario had not been so forgetful.

With great contempt Malvolio relates what Olivia wishes Cesario to tell Duke Orsino. He is to make it clear that she will have nothing to do with the duke. Cesario must never return with any more of Orsino's messages, unless he comes to tell Olivia how Orsino took this rejection.

Y

Viola realises that Olivia is in love with Cesario

Cesario is put off by Malvolio's arrogant and scornful manner, and refuses the ring. The outraged Malvolio throws the ring on the ground and departs.

Alone on the stage, Viola reflects on what has happened. All the evidence seems to suggest that Olivia has fallen in love with 'Cesario'. Olivia obviously sent Malvolio with the ring as a trick in order to lure the messenger back.

Viola pities Olivia. The lady might just as well 'love a dream' as a woman disguised as a man. Viola realises that the situation is very complicated: Viola loves Orsino, her master, as much as he loves Olivia; Olivia mistakenly dotes on Cesario, who is really a woman, Viola. She cannot think of a solution. She hopes that time will unravel this 'hard' knot and the scene ends.

Scene 3

Late at night in Olivia's house Sir Toby Belch and Sir Andrew Aguecheek are having a drinking session.

Feste, the clown, is also up late and he comes in, adding his own word-play and nonsense to this comic scene. Sir Andrew is delighted with the clown's fooling, and knowing he has a sweet voice asks him to sing. Sir Toby requests a love song.

Feste sings a song, 'O Mistress Mine'. After some more joking, the three decide to sing together. They make a terrible sound and Olivia's servant, Maria, rushes in to complain at their 'caterwauling'.

Malvolio breaks up the party

Maria begs them to keep the noise down, but they are too drunk to take anything or anybody seriously. Just as Sir Toby begins a new song, an indignant Malvolio appears, and scolds them for their lack of manners and respect for others. If Sir Toby will not stop this rowdiness he must leave at once. Before he goes off, Malvolio also warns Maria that he will be reporting her part in the unruliness to her mistress.

Maria plans to make a fool of Malvolio

Maria proposes a plan to make the pompous Malvolio look a fool. She will forge a love letter in Olivia's handwriting, which is often mistaken for hers, and this letter will contain an admiring description of Malvolio. Malvolio will find it and foolishly believe that Olivia is in love with him. Maria suggests that Sir Toby and Sir Andrew spy on Malvolio to watch how he interprets the letter.

Sir Toby and Sir Andrew are delighted at the chance to make Malvolio look foolish.

Scene 4

Duke Orsino and 'Cesario' talk about love

Duke Orsino is with his courtiers in his palace. He calls for music to be played. He tells Cesario that he would particularly like to hear a song that was performed during the previous evening; 'That old and antic song' (line 3) seemed to soothe him far more than any of the superficial songs of the present time. Curio is sent to bring Feste, the clown, to sing and while they are waiting the duke talks to Cesario against a background of the old tune played by the musicians.

The duke tells Cesario to remember him if he should ever fall in love. For he, Orsino, is the typical true lover, lively and playful in all emotions except when he has in mind the 'constant image' of his beloved. Cesario hints that he already knows something about love and when Orsino asks him if he has ever been in love, Cesario cautiously admits that he has. The duke becomes curious about the woman who has attracted him. He questions the youth about what she is like, her appearance and age.

Cesario says that the woman is very like Orsino, both in personality and age. Orsino is scornful: this woman is unworthy of Cesario and certainly too old. A woman should take an older man, he advises, because women become emotionally mature earlier than men and an older man is more likely to satisfy a woman's needs. We young men may think highly of ourselves in love, he says, but our emotions are unstable, 'more giddy and unfirm' (line 33), more easily worn out than those of women. Orsino recommends Cesario find himself a virgin in the first bloom of youthful beauty. She will keep his love alive for longer.

Curio returns with Feste and Orsino instructs the clown to sing the song. He tells Cesario to note that the song is 'old and plain' (line 43) and used to be sung by both old women and carefree young maids. Its theme is the innocence of love.

The lover in this melancholy song is a young man whose heart has been broken by a 'fair cruel maid' (line 54). He wants to die and be buried without friends or other mourners so that no one will know where his bones are laid, 'O where / Sad true lover never find my grave, / To weep there' (lines 64–6). The deep sadness of the song reflects the duke's mood; he is pleased with Feste's performance and pays him for it.

Everybody except the duke and Cesario leave and Orsino tells him that he must return to Olivia and convince her that his love for her is truly noble. He is not impressed by Olivia's wealth and possessions – his soul loves her for what nature has given her, 'that miracle and queen of gems' (line 86), her beauty. And what, asks Cesario, if she cannot love you? Orsino replies that he will not take no for an answer.

Cesario tells Orsino that he must accept her refusal. After all, if some lady was in love with the duke, and he did not love her in return, he would be forced to tell her and he would expect her to accept it. Orsino does not believe that women can love as passionately as men. He thinks women simply do not have the physical capacity for deep feeling; they quickly become sick of love as they are too greedy for it in the first place. Orsino's love, by comparison, is 'as hungry as the sea' (line 101) and like the ocean can absorb far more. He is convinced that there is no comparison between the love any woman could feel for him and the feelings he has for Olivia.

Cesario, who of course is really Viola and loves Orsino, replies that he knows only too well how much women are able to love men. Their hearts, he says, are as 'true' as 'we' men. He knows this because his father had a daughter who loved a man quite as much as he might love Orsino if he, Cesario, were a woman. Orsino is intrigued by this and asks what happened to the girl. She 'never told her love' (line 111), says Cesario, but pined away hiding her feelings from her beloved. Her concealed love consumed all her youth. He tells Orsino that 'we' men may talk a lot about our feelings, but we talk more than we actually feel. And, Orsino asks, did your sister die of her love? Cesario answers with a riddle: 'I am all the daughters of my father's house, / And all the brothers too' (lines 120–1). On this mysterious note the scene ends. Orsino dispatches Cesario to Olivia. He is to tell her that the duke's love cannot be denied.

Comment

This scene provides a strong contrast to the previous one. The change of mood is established by music – from the 'caterwauling' in Olivia's house to the 'old and antic'

Viola's
disguise
means that
the audience
knows much
more than
Orsino here;
read the
scene from
Orsino's
point of view
and then
from the
audience's

song in Orsino's – and by the seriousness of the conversation between Orsino and Cesario.

We are more interested in Viola's emotions here than in Orsino's. She speaks in the 'fictional' role of a man, Cesario, but she also tries to express indirectly her real feelings as a woman who is secretly in love with Orsino.

Look at the way the scene is constructed. The two dialogues between Orsino and Cesario are separated by Feste's song about unrequited love (loving someone who does not love you). The theme of the song reflects the emotional situation of both Orsino and Viola.

The ending of the scene tells the audience that there will soon be another meeting between Olivia and Cesario (Viola).

Scene 5

Maria
has forged
a letter

In Olivia's garden Sir Toby, Sir Andrew and one of her servants, Fabian, meet together to see the trick they are playing on Malvolio. Fabian is keen to watch this 'sport' since he also has a grudge against the Puritan: Malvolio has reported him to Olivia for bear-baiting, which was a popular sport in Elizabethan times. Sir Toby tells him that they will soon be turning Malvolio into an angry bear himself.

Soon Maria arrives with the 'bait', the forged letter, and she tells them to hide themselves in the 'box-tree'. Malvolio is approaching and Maria drops the letter on the path where he will find it easily. Malvolio will be caught because of his vanity, she assures them before she leaves.

Malvolio enters. He is engrossed in thoughts of Olivia and the possibility that she might love him. After all, Maria once told him that his mistress admired him. And Olivia herself admitted that if she should ever fall in love again, it would be with someone very like Malvolio. He knows that she respects him far more than any of her other servants.

To the indignation of the eavesdroppers, Malvolio fantasises about being married to Olivia, being 'Count Malvolio'. He remembers the story of a noble lady who married one of her servants. Malvolio has no difficulty picturing himself as a loving husband, dressed in velvet, surrounded by servants. And it would be a special pleasure to be able to summon Sir Toby Belch and give him orders. He would instruct Olivia's uncle to give up his drunkenness and tell him that he is wasting too much time with a foolish knight, 'One Sir Andrew' (line 80).

Then Malvolio catches sight of the letter. He picks it up and begins to read it out loud, utterly convinced it is in Olivia's handwriting. The phrases used in the letter are typical of Olivia and the note has her stamp, so it must be from her. There is a love poem inside and the first verse says that only God knows the man whom the writer loves and no one else must know who it is. If only this person were Malvolio! The second verse persuades him that it is indeed him whom she loves because it includes the words 'I may command where I adore' (line 106). He, after all, is Olivia's steward and she may command him: 'I serve her, she is my lady' (line 117). The first part is all quite logical, but what of the letters M.O.A.I. which end the poem? Malvolio soon takes them to signify him, since all the letters are in his name.

Malvolio then finds a prose letter enclosed with the poem. It is this letter that finally convinces him that Olivia loves him. The letter says that if it should by chance fall into her beloved's hands, then he should consider the fact that the woman who loves him is, through fate, of a higher social rank than him. He should not be afraid of this 'greatness' – 'Some are born great, some achieve greatness, and some have greatness thrust upon 'em' (lines 145–6). The author of the letter writes that Fate calls on him to take the initiative for he is being made a very generous offer. He should be bold, cast off his usual clothes and start wearing yellow stockings and cross garters. He should be rude to servants and go about talking of important, high-flown subjects. Unless he does all these things he will still be thought of as a mere steward, a servant who is 'not worthy to touch Fortune's fingers' (lines 156–7). The letter is signed 'The Fortunate Unhappy'.

Malvolio is overjoyed. He tells himself he will do all that has been 'commended'. He will be 'proud', he will treat Sir Toby with contempt, he will have nothing to do with low-born people, he will be exactly the man described in the letter. For it is as clear as daylight that Olivia wrote it, and nothing makes this plainer than the reference to yellow stockings and cross garters, for Olivia has recently admired his stockings and obviously wants him to continue wearing them.

A postscript to the letter which Malvolio reads out contains more encouragement. It says that by now he must surely realise who the writer is and, if he is prepared to love her, he should show this by smiling in her presence, smiling all the time.

Malvolio leaves, and Sir Toby, Sir Andrew and Fabian emerge from their hiding place. Soon Maria also joins them. They are all very pleased with the trick which she has played on Malvolio. Sir Toby especially is full of admiration and claims he would marry her and 'ask no other dowry … but such another jest' (lines 184–5). He tells Maria that with her cleverness she has completely conquered him. The letter has put Malvolio 'in such a dream' (line 193) that when he wakes up to reality he will go mad. Maria tells them that if they want to see the 'fruits of the sport' (line 197) they must watch for Malvolio's next encounter with Olivia. He is sure to appear in yellow stockings (a colour she hates) and cross garters ('a fashion she detests' – line 200). And Malvolio's endless smiling is bound to make the melancholic Olivia extremely annoyed.

All the characters leave the stage keenly looking forward to Malvolio's humiliation.

|Comment   This scene provides another strong contrast and takes us into the comic **sub-plot**, the trick played on Malvolio. We meet a new character, Fabian, who offers another

reason for the attack on Malvolio: the steward has reported him for bear-baiting, a sport Puritans strongly disapproved of.

When Malvolio enters, he is already absorbed in ambitious fantasies, so his conceit makes him an easy target for the tricksters.

The dramatic convention of **soliloquy** (see Literary Terms), where a character speaks his thoughts alone, is exploited to full comic effect here.

The letter is signed 'The Fortunate Unhappy', a typical Elizabethan **oxymoron** (see Literary Terms) – a phrase that combines one idea with its opposite.

Maria has obviously written the letter knowing very well what her mistress dislikes; she clearly understands Malvolio's character as well and the letter plays upon his weaknesses.

The yellow stockings and cross garters mentioned in the letter would have been considered ridiculously unfashionable in Elizabethan times.

Test (Act II)

a Fill in the blanks

Sebastian has been rescued by .... who is an enemy of Orsino. .... decides to go to the duke's court and .... follows him.

.... and .... are getting drunk and singing. They are joined by .... and .... After .... has interrupted their party and told them off, ... proposes to forge a letter in ....'s handwriting. It will contain an admiring description of .... and she will leave it for him to find.

At ....'s court, ... sings a song and Orsino and .... talk about love. Maria places the letter in ....'s garden and .... finds it. ....,... and .... and .... watch from behind a hedge. .... reads the letter out loud. He becomes convinced that .... loves him and vows to do everything that she commands.

b Give modern words for these words used by Shakespeare

1 distemper (II.1.5)
2 fadge (II.2.32)
3 monster (II.2.33)
4 stoup (II.3.14)
5 breast (II.3.19)

6 pranks (II.4.87)
7 motion (II.4.99)
8 fustian (II.5.10)
9 strange (II.5.171)

C Quiz

1 What is the name of Sebastian's helper

2 Who has Olivia fallen for?

3 What are Sir Toby and Sir Andrew doing in scene 3?

4 Who interrupts the party?

5 Who thinks up the trick against Malvolio

6 Who sings a song for Orsino?

7 What is it about?

8 Who spies on Malvolio in the garden

9 What does Malvolio find in the letter?

10 What does Sir Toby promise Maria?

a Antonio Sebastian Antonio Sir Toby Sir Andrew Feste Maria
Malvolio Maria Olivia Malvolio Orsino Feste Cesario (Viola)
Olivia Malvolio Fabian Sir Andrew Sir Toby Malvolio Olivia

b 1 infect 2 turn out 3 both 'man' and 'woman' 4 drinking vessel
5 singing voice 6 adorns 7 emotion 8 high-flown 9 aloof

c 1 Antonio 2 Cesario 3 drinking and singing 4 Malvolio
5 Maria 6 Feste 7 love 8 Sir Toby, Sir Andrew and Fabian
9 a poem and instructions 10 to marry her

Act III

Scene 1

'Cesario' has come to see Olivia

Still in disguise as Cesario, Viola has once more come to Olivia's house to tell her of Orsino's love. In the garden she meets Feste, the clown, who is playing on the pipe and drum. They indulge in some light-hearted witty conversation until Cesario points out that people who play so cleverly with words, as Feste does, may soon give them obscene double meanings. He asks Feste if he is Olivia's fool and the jester replies that he is not: 'She will keep no fool, sir, till she be married' (lines 33–4). Rather, he is her 'corrupter of words' (line 37).

Feste is respectful towards Cesario, while at the same time demonstrating that he is his equal in wit. And Cesario is pleased to have a bit of fun before the serious business which he has come to perform; he pays the clown who goes inside to announce his presence.

While waiting, Cesario reflects that a fool must be both intelligent and sensitive to perform his role well. The fool must be aware of the mood and social status of each person he makes fun of, making sure his wit is suitable for the occasion and not just letting his jokes fly anywhere. To be a good fool, concludes Cesario, is as difficult as 'a wise man's art' (line 67).

At this point Sir Toby and Sir Andrew enter. The two knights are terribly impressed by Cesario's manners, and Sir Andrew in particular is struck by his courtly language: 'That youth's a rare courtier' (line 88) he observes.

When Olivia arrives she orders all the others to leave so that she can be alone with Cesario. Straightaway she asks for his hand, but he keeps his distance, reminding her that he is her servant because, being the servant of Orsino, who is her servant in love, he, Cesario, is therefore her servant. Olivia is dismissive of such complicated reasoning and wishes that Orsino thought nothing of her. She does not want to speak of the duke. Her thoughts are all on Cesario and she would much prefer it if he had come to woo her for himself.

Olivia reveals her love for 'Cesario' She then confesses that she sent Malvolio with the ring simply as an excuse to make Cesario return to her. She is unhappy and wants him to think well of her, even though she thinks he must despise her for being so frank about her feelings. All Cesario can say is that he pities her. That at least is close to love, suggests Olivia. Cesario disagrees: we often pity our enemies, he says. Olivia cannot conceal her disappointment at being rejected by Cesario, but she assures him that she will not pursue the subject further. Whoever marries Cesario will certainly be marrying a 'proper man' (line 135) she says.

As Cesario prepares to leave he asks Olivia one last time if she has any message for Duke Orsino. Olivia pleads with him to stay and tell her what he thinks of her. They both confess that they are not what they appear to be, then Olivia breaks into an impassioned declaration of her love for Cesario. No woman ever has or ever will conquer my heart, Cesario informs her, and says goodbye. Olivia begs him to come again in the hope that one day he may be able to love her.

Comment This scene continues the events of Act II scene 4 in which Orsino sent Cesario to Olivia. The scenes of the main romantic plot alternate with those of the **sub-plot** (see Literary Terms). By starting this scene with some of the comic characters, Shakespeare begins to bring the two plots together.

Cesario's style of speaking impresses Sir Andrew. Later the knight's jealousy will be made worse by this, resulting in the pretend duel between the two (Act III scene 4).

The clown demonstrates his wit, his ability to make **puns** (see Literary Terms) and to be Olivia's 'corrupter of words' (line 37).

The dialogue (lines 140–6) emphasises the complications that the disguise has caused: both Cesario and Olivia are 'not what they are' – Cesario is really a woman; Olivia thinks she is in love with a man.

Scene 2 Sir Andrew, Sir Toby and Fabian are in Olivia's house discussing Sir Andrew's attempt to win the affections of Olivia. He believes that Olivia cares more for Cesario than she does for him. Sir Andrew has seen them together in the orchard, and it was clear that Olivia is in love with the youth from the way she behaved. Fabian tells him that she was just trying to make Sir Andrew jealous and really Olivia wanted Sir Andrew to march up

Sir Toby and Fabian persuade Sir Andrew to challenge 'Cesario'

to them and insult Cesario, and then he 'should have banged the youth into a dumbness' (line 21). As it is, the knight has lost a perfect opportunity to demonstrate his bravery and he must redeem himself by some act of courage.

Sir Andrew decides to challenge Cesario to a duel. When the foolish Aguecheek has gone, Sir Toby and Fabian laugh at this new practical joke they are playing.

Maria arrives to inform them that Malvolio is obeying 'every point of the letter' (line 74). He is wearing a pair of yellow stockings and smiling all the time. She leads them off to enjoy the result of their practical joke.

Scene 3

Sebastian and Antonio are in Illyria

Viola's twin brother, Sebastian, and Antonio the sea captain walk in the street near Orsino's palace. Antonio has followed Sebastian into Illyria because he did not want him to wander alone in a strange country.

Sebastian is very grateful to Antonio. Antonio hands Sebastian a purse containing money and they agree to meet later at an inn called The Elephant.

Scene 4

Olivia is in her garden anxiously expecting Cesario, whom she has invited to visit her. She wonders where Malvolio is. His serious and polite manner would soothe her. Maria informs her that Malvolio is on his way to see her, but warns her mistress that he has become 'very strange' (line 8) and is probably possessed by the devil.

Malvolio behaves very strangely

With a foolish smile on his face, Malvolio enters. The steward has shed his normally dark clothes and is wearing yellow stockings. He is far from the 'sad and civil' (line 5) Malvolio she is used to, having transformed himself into a ludicrous fawning courtier, smiling inanely and blowing her kisses, and making suggestive references to what he believes to be her feelings towards him. He pays no attention to her expressions of surprise and confusion and continues to quote lines from the forged letter. Olivia tries to get some sense out of him – what is this talk about 'greatness'? – but Malvolio continues to ramble on, to such a degree that Olivia concludes he is suffering from some kind of 'midsummer madness' (line 55).

The arrival of Cesario is announced and before she goes off to see him Olivia instructs Maria to take charge of the deranged Malvolio. She asks that other members of her household look after him too, including Sir Toby.

Left alone on the stage, Malvolio remembers how the letter told him to treat Sir Toby – ('be opposite with a kinsman' (line 69) – and when the knight enters, accompanied by Fabian and Maria, he is rude to them all. Eventually they are driven to exasperation by Malvolio's behaviour. After he has left they plan to have him locked up in a dark room, the normal place for Elizabethan lunatics. Sir Toby reminds them that Olivia already thinks that Malvolio is mad, so they can carry their joke a little further, 'for our pleasure and his penance' (lines 138–9).

At this point Sir Andrew Aguecheek enters, clutching the challenge he has just written to Cesario. He is very proud of this piece of writing and Sir Toby reads it out loud. The absurd language is full of clumsy and obscure phrases. Sir Toby says he will personally deliver the challenge himself. Maria informs them that Cesario is at present with Olivia, so this would be an excellent time to hand it over.

Sir Toby advises Sir Andrew to approach Cesario from behind, with his sword drawn and swearing horribly.

This will make the knight look very tough and manly, far more than any actual deed of courage. Sir Andrew goes off to do battle with Cesario.

Aware that a challenge written in such absurd language would not frighten the well-bred Cesario, but simply make him think it came from an illiterate idiot, Sir Toby decides to deliver the challenge verbally. He will play off Aguecheek and Cesario against one another, making each so frightened 'that they will kill one another by the look, like cockatrices' (lines 196–7).

Just as the jokers are leaving the stage, Olivia enters with Cesario. Sir Toby decides to leave them together for a while to give him time to think up 'some horrid message for a challenge' (lines 201–2).

A short conversation follows in which Olivia continues to 'woo' Cesario. Olivia gives him a jewelled brooch containing a miniature portrait of herself, and after telling him to return to her the next day, she leaves.

Sir Toby makes Sir Andrew and 'Cesario' believe they must fight a duel

Sir Toby and Fabian then return and Sir Toby tells Cesario to prepare to defend himself, for his 'interceptor', Sir Andrew, is waiting for him in the orchard. He must draw his sword quickly for Sir Andrew is a 'skilful, and deadly' opponent (line 227).

Cesario can think of no man who might want to fight him; he has offended no one. Sir Toby proceeds to paint a picture of Sir Andrew as a fearsome fighter, a 'devil' who has killed three men already in private disputes. Cesario becomes very alarmed and makes to return to Olivia's house to seek protection, but Sir Toby urges him on to fight – 'strip your sword stark naked' (line 254).

Cesario implores Sir Toby to go to this knight and discover what offence he has given and Sir Toby exits, pretending to do this, leaving the frightened courtier with Fabian. Fabian leads him off to 'the most skilful, bloody, and fatal opposite that you could possibly have found in any part of Illyria' (lines 270–2).

Antonio arrives and is arrested

Sir Toby and Sir Andrew enter, and Aguecheek is soon terrified by Sir Toby's description of Cesario's ferocity. He offers to give Cesario his horse 'Capilet' in order to pacify him, and when Cesario returns the two 'opponents' are provoked to draw their swords.

Suddenly, Antonio enters. He sees Cesario and mistakenly believes it is his friend, Sebastian, Viola's twin brother. He calls on Sir Andrew to put up his sword, unless he wants to fight Antonio. Just as Sir Toby draws *his* sword and prepares to fight Antonio, a troop of officers arrive on the scene. They have come for Antonio. He has been recognised in the street and Orsino has sent them to arrest him.

Antonio appeals to Cesario for help and asks him to return his money. Cesario, who at this point naturally knows nothing of Antonio's mistake, denies he has been given any money by the man. But out of charity he offers to give him some money, since he has shown him such kindness. Antonio is upset because his friend seems ungrateful. He tells the crowd that he once saved this youth from 'the jaws of death' (line 369) and then served him with great devotion. He turns on Cesario and curses him: 'But O how vile an idol proves this god! / Thou hast, Sebastian, done good features shame' (lines 374–5). The officers take him away.

Viola hopes her brother may be alive

When Viola (Cesario) hears the name 'Sebastian' she begins to hope that Antonio's mistake is a sign that her brother is still alive. Surely, she thinks, it is possible that Antonio has indeed saved her brother from the

Y

shipwreck and because of her disguise has thought she was him: 'For him I imitate' (line 393). She prays for this to be true and leaves the stage. Sir Toby and Fabian squeeze out the last drop of fun from their joke by convincing the foolish Sir Andrew that Cesario is a coward and has run away. They urge him to follow the page and 'cuff him soundly' (line 401).

Comment

This scene is one of the two longest scenes in the entire play. It can be divided up into several sections featuring different groups of characters and making use of the mistaken identities and deceptions which Shakespeare has been preparing in the previous scenes. The deceived or mistaken characters are Malvolio, Olivia, Viola, Sir Andrew and Antonio.

When Malvolio enters, the change in his appearance is very dramatic and very funny. Much of the comedy comes from his total confidence that Olivia knows what he is talking about when he quotes from the letter. Maria at this point is the only one on the stage who, like the audience, knows the truth of the joke.

Sir Toby takes an important role in the scene. He devises some more fun between Sir Andrew and Cesario, knowing full well that neither will come to any harm.

An additional absurdity is the entrance of Antonio, who attempts to defend 'Sebastian' (Viola disguised as Cesario) and ends up drawing swords with Sir Toby.

We sense at the end of the scene that the various elements of the plot's confusions will soon be unravelled. For example, when Viola hears her brother's name it marks a turning point, even though the 'knot' will not be untied until after Sebastian has been mistaken for Cesario.

Test (Act III)

a Fill in
the blanks

.... confesses to .... that she has fallen
in love with 'him'. She is rejected.

Sir .... sees them together and becomes
jealous. He is persuaded by Sir .... to challenge
.... to a duel.

When .... sees .... she thinks he
has gone mad because he is wearing ....
.... and .... and is smiling
all the time. She orders him to be locked up in a
....

Sir .... and .... are brought together
and draw their swords. .... enters and thinks
.... is .... He threatens to attack Sir
.... and Sir .... Some officers arrive
and arrest .... , who calls Cesario by the name
of ....

b Give modern words for these
words used by Shakespeare

1 constant (III.1.57)
2 grize (III.1.126)
3 clause (III.1.155)
4 Brownist (III.2.30)
5 cubiculo (III.2.50)

6 spleen (III.2.65)
7 jealousy (III.3.8)
8 limed (III.4.74)
9 private (III.4.90)
10 Hob, nob (III.4.242)

C Quiz

1 Who does Cesario meet in Olivia's garden?

2 What does Olivia confess to Cesario?

3 Who spies on Olivia and Cesario?

4 What does Sir Andrew do?

5 What is Malvolio wearing when he meets Olivia

6 Where is Malvolio taken?

7 Who fights a duel

8 Who interrupts the duel?

9 Who does Antonio think Cesario is

10 What makes Viola think her brother is still alive?

Answers

C 1 Feste   2 she loves him   3 Sir Andrew   4 he challenges Cesario to a duel   5 yellow stockings and cross garters   6 to a dark room   7 Sir Andrew   8 Antonio   9 Sebastian   10 Antonio calls her Sebastian and Cesario

b 1 explain   2 step   3 premise   4 Puritan   5 little bedroom   6 laughter   7 anxiety   8 caught   9 own company   10 Have or have not

a Olivia   Cesario   Andrew   Toby   Cesario   Sebastian   Antonio   Toby   Andrew   Olivia   Malvolio
yellow stockings   cross garters   dark room   Andrew   Cesario
Antonio   Cesario   Sebastian   Toby   Andrew   Antonio   Sebastian

Act IV

Scene 1

In the street near Olivia's house, Feste, the clown, has mistaken Sebastian for Cesario and is insisting that Olivia has sent for him.

Sir Andrew hits Sebastian thinking he is 'Cesario'

Sir Andrew, Sir Toby and Fabian enter. They too believe that Sebastian is Cesario and Sir Andrew hits him. In return, Sebastian gives Sir Andrew a sound beating. Feste immediately goes off to report this to Olivia. Sir Toby decides to intervene and grabs hold of Sebastian. They draw their swords and are about to fight, when Olivia enters.

Olivia also thinks Sebastian is 'Cesario'

Olivia, also believing that Sebastian is Cesario, asks him to go into the house. She scolds Sir Toby for his lack of manners and tells him to get out of her sight: 'Rudesby, be gone!' (line 49). Sir Toby, Sir Andrew and Fabian exit.

When she is alone with Sebastian, Olivia apologises for her uncle's behaviour. Sebastian is amazed at all this. He is being wooed by a beautiful woman whom he has never seen before. Is he mad? Or is he dreaming? Whichever is the case, he happily agrees to do whatever she asks.

Scene 2

KEY SCENE

Malvolio is locked in a dark room

Malvolio has been locked in a dark room to cure him of his 'midsummer madness'. Maria and Feste, the clown, enter and play one final trick on him: Feste dresses up as a priest, 'Sir Topas', who will interview Malvolio. Maria goes off to fetch Sir Toby.

When 'Sir Topas' talks to Malvolio he uses obscure Latin phrases and nonsensical arguments about philosophy. The steward is 'relieved to hear a priest's voice' and thinks he will soon be released. This does not happen: he will remain in 'darkness' for some time. 'Sir Topas' leaves Malvolio crying for help.

Sir Toby, who has been brought back by Maria, tells the clown to speak to Malvolio in his normal voice. Sir Toby wants to put an end to this 'knavery' because he is out of favour with Olivia. He is worried that his niece will turn him out of the house.

Feste goes back into the dark room, this time singing a popular song in his own voice. When Malvolio recognises him, he asks for 'a candle, and pen, ink, and paper' (line 84) so that he can send a message to Olivia.

In the darkness Feste makes Malvolio believe there are two people present by sometimes using his own voice and sometimes that of 'Sir Topas'. Malvolio insists that he is not insane and that he has been 'notoriously abused' (line 90). The clown goes off, singing, to fetch the writing materials.

Comment	As before, a disguise is used to create comedy.

Feste wears a parson's black gown here. This is the colour normally associated with Malvolio, who in contrast is dressed in bright colours. This reversal provides a visual symbol of just how thoroughly he has been humiliated.

Feste says 'there is no darkness but ignorance' (lines 43–4) and Malvolio's ignorance has been exposed in the scene. He was ignorant to think that Olivia could ever love him in the first place.

Scene 3

Sebastian agrees to marry Olivia

Sebastian sits alone in Olivia's garden reflecting on what has happened.

Olivia enters with a priest. She asks Sebastian to go with her straight away to her private chapel so they can be married. The marriage will be kept secret for the time being. Sebastian agrees wholeheartedly and they exit.

Test (Act IV)

a Fill in the blanks

Sebastian is attacked by Sir .... because he thinks he is .... also thinks Sebastian is .... and scolds her uncle, ... , for threatening him.

.... and .... play another trick on .... while he is locked up in the dark room.

Sir Toby brings the trickery to a halt and .... agrees to help .... explain that he is not really mad.

Olivia calls for a .... and takes .... off so they can be married. Olivia still thinks he is ....

b Give modern words for these words used by Shakespeare

1 cockney (IV.1.15)
2 Lethe (IV.1.61)
3 Bonas dies (IV.2.13)
4 puzzled (IV.2.44)
5 Advise you (IV.2.97)

6 shent (IV.2.108)
7 credit (IV.3.6)
8 deceivable (IV.23.24)
9 chantry (IV.3.24)
10 whiles (IV.3.29)

C Quiz

1 Who is attacked by Sir Andrew?

2 What does Sebastian do to Sir Andrew?

3 Who does Olivia think Sebastian is?

4 What is the name of the character Feste pretends to be

5 Who stops the joke against Malvolio

6 How does Feste help Malvolio?

7 Whom does Olivia marry

8 Whom does Olivia think she is marrying?

Answers

C 1 Sebastian   2 he beats him   3 Cesario   4 Sir Topas   5 Sir Toby
6 he brings him a pen, ink and paper   7 Sebastian   8 Cesario

b 1 feeble thing   2 river of oblivion   3 good day   4 lost   5 be careful
6 rebuked   7 report   8 deceptive   9 part of church or chapel   10 until

a Andrew   Cesario   Olivia   Cesario   Sir Toby   Cesario   Feste   Maria
Malvolio   Feste   Malvolio   priest   Sebastian   Cesario

Act V

Scene 1

KEY SCENE

In the street outside Olivia's house, Feste is on his way to deliver Malvolio's letter. He is stopped by Fabian who tries unsuccessfully to persuade the clown to let him see the letter.

The duke enters with Cesario (Viola), Curio and some noble men. The clown entertains them with witty conversation and Duke Orsino is pleased by this – he gives Feste a gold coin and orders him to announce to Olivia that he has come to see her.

While they are waiting Antonio is brought in by some officers. Cesario tells the duke that this is the man who intervened in his duel with Sir Andrew. Orsino recognises Antonio's face, even though the last time he saw it, it was 'besmear'd / As black as Vulcan, in the smoke of war' (lines 50–1). Antonio had been the captain of a tiny pirate ship which, in spite of its size, had fought heroically against the most powerful of the duke's vessels.

Antonio protests that although he was at that time Orsino's enemy, he was never a pirate. He goes on to explain how he has come to be in Illyria, and he points at Cesario who he still believes is Sebastian. He claims he has been bewitched by the 'ingrateful boy' (line 75) who is standing at Orsino's side. I rescued him from a shipwreck, he says, and cared for him with love and devotion for three months. In return, complains Antonio, he has denied he knows me and refused to give me back my money.

Olivia enters with her attendants. Orsino tells Antonio that Cesario has been his servant for the last three months and therefore Antonio's talk is 'madness'.

Olivia is annoyed. She asks Orsino what she can do for him and then accuses Cesario of failing to keep an appointment with her. Orsino becomes very angry with Olivia and his frustration makes him turn on Cesario, whom he knows Olivia loves. He threatens to kill him out of spite for Olivia. Cesario consents to follow Orsino and submit to whatever fate he has in store for 'him', for 'he' loves Orsino more than his life, 'More, by all mores, than e'er I shall love wife' (line 134). Olivia is horrified, and she calls for the priest who married her to Cesario (in reality to Sebastian). The priest enters and confirms that he did indeed marry them only two hours before. An enraged Orsino turns on Cesario and orders 'him' to leave his sight forever. Cesario (Viola) tries to protest but is stopped by Olivia.

Sir Andrew enters crying out for a surgeon. He and Sir Toby have been wounded by Cesario, he claims. Sir Andrew's head has been broken and Sir Toby has a 'bloody coxcomb' (line 174). Cesario (Viola) protests that 'he' did not hurt Sir Andrew when the knight drew his sword, but merely spoke politely to him. Drunk and bleeding, Sir Toby comes in with the clown, Feste, who tells him that the surgeon cannot come because he is drunk. Sir Toby curses the surgeon: 'I hate a drunken rogue' (line 199), he says.

Olivia soon puts a stop to all this 'havoc' by sending Sir Toby off to bed and he departs with Sir Andrew. The clown and Fabian follow them.

Sebastian enters

Sebastian, the cause of all this confusion, now enters. He apologises to Olivia for injuring her uncle but explains that he would have had to do the same even if it had been his own brother, in order to protect himself. He notices that Olivia is looking at him strangely and thinks she is very offended, but like Orsino and Antonio, Olivia is simply amazed at the extraordinary likeness between Sebastian and Cesario. And when Sebastian sees Cesario he too is astonished to see someone who looks so like himself – 'Do I stand there?' (line 224) – and asks him if they are related. Cesario (Viola) tells him that he looks very like a twin brother called Sebastian who drowned in a 'watery tomb' (line 232), and that Cesario's father was called 'Sebastian' also. Sebastian could be this brother's ghost.

Sebastian and Viola recognise each other

As soon as Sebastian and Viola (Cesario) realise they had the same father, Viola reveals herself as Sebastian's lost sister. She says that she can confirm this by taking Sebastian to the sea captain who has been keeping her clothes all this while, the same sea captain who helped her to disguise herself as 'Cesario' and serve Duke Orsino as a messenger in the 'business' of his wooing Olivia.

Sebastian informs Olivia that she has been 'mistook' and would have been married to a virgin girl if she had married 'Cesario' but since she in fact married him, Sebastian, she has married a virgin youth ('a maid and man').

Duke Orsino and Viola will be married

The duke turns to Viola and reminds her that, as 'Cesario', she had claimed many times that she would never love a woman as much as she loved him. He takes her hand and asks to see her dressed in her 'woman's weeds' (line 271). Viola replies that the captain who has her clothes is at present being kept in prison by Malvolio.

Olivia calls for Malvolio to be brought in so that the captain can be released and Feste returns carrying the steward's letter. Olivia orders the clown to read the letter out loud, but the affected voice he puts on is too distracting, so she asks Fabian to read it. The duke does not believe a true madman could have written such a letter and Olivia tells Fabian to bring in Malvolio.

Malvolio arrives clutching the love letter which he believes Olivia had written to him. Olivia instantly recognises her servant, Maria's, handwriting. She sees that a very clever practical joke has been played on Malvolio, and promises him that when more is known about it, he shall be both 'plaintiff and judge' (line 353) in the case.

The joke played on Malvolio is revealed

Fabian describes the plot to make a fool of Malvolio and explains why they wanted to get revenge on the steward. He says that Maria wrote the letter at Sir Toby's suggestion and the knight was so pleased by it that he has married her 'in recompense'.

Olivia expresses pity for the 'poor fool' (line 368) Malvolio and Feste teases him, repeating some of the phrases from the letter and the 'Sir Topas' episode. He

tells Malvolio that this is how time brings revenge. The enraged Malvolio exits, threatening his own revenge on all of them.

Duke Orsino then promises a happy union between Viola and himself, for when she has exchanged her male disguise for women's clothes, she will be 'Orsino's mistress, and his fancy's queen' (line 387).

All the characters leave except Feste, the clown, who sings a final song to end the play.

Comment

The conversation between Orsino and the clown establishes a light-hearted mood. Feste is carrying Malvolio's letter to Olivia which will later resolve the sub-plot (see Literary Terms) of the practical jokes that have been played on him.

The confusions caused by the various mistaken identities are brought to a climax after the introduction of Antonio. He accuses Cesario of betraying him. Then Olivia, also believing Cesario is Sebastian, accuses him of betraying their marriage vows. And Orsino accuses Cesario of having betrayed him.

Shakespeare makes the audience wait a little longer to sort out these mistakes by bringing on Sir Andrew and Sir Toby, bruised and bleeding from their encounter with Sebastian. They in turn accuse the disguised Viola of assaulting them. Their description of 'Cesario' as a 'very devil incardinate' (line 179) makes a humorous contrast to the civilised and gentle Viola known to the audience.

The appearance of Sebastian solves all the mysteries. When reading the play it is important to visualise this moment and imagine both twins dressed as men and therefore impossible for the other characters to tell apart.

This final part of the scene focuses on Sebastian, because Viola must gradually come to recognise her lost brother, just as Sebastian himself must recognise his lost sister through her disguise as 'Cesario'.

As often happens in **romantic comedy** (see Literary Terms) all the main characters end up partnered off – Olivia with Sebastian, Orsino with Viola, and we learn that even Sir Toby has married Maria.

Only Malvolio is left alone outside this happy conclusion: he is angry and resentful, having learned the facts of his deception.

Test (Act V)

a Fill in the blanks

Antonio explains that he is not a pirate, and tells how he rescued ...., who he thinks has now disowned him. He confuses .... for .... when he accuses him.

Olivia rejects .... and tells him she has married .... Orsino threatens to kill .... to spite Olivia.

Sir Andrew and Sir Toby claim that .... has assaulted them. When Sebastian enters, ... recognises him and reveals her true identity.

Olivia sends for .... and he finds out how he has been tricked.

At the end, Sir Toby has married .... , Olivia is happy to be married to .... , and .... promises to marry ....

The play finishes with a song sung by ....

b Give modern words for these words used by Shakespeare

1	baubling (V.1.53)	6	state (V.1.62)
2	bottom (V.1.55)	7	bias (V.1.258)
3	fraught (V.1.59)	8	glass (V.1.263)
4	Candy (V.1.59)	9	convents (V.1.381)
5	shame (V.1.62)	10	fancy's (V.1.387)

C Quiz

1 Who intercepts Feste when he is delivering the letter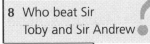

2 Who entertains the Duke when he is waiting for Olivia?

3 When was the last time that Orsino encountered Antonio?

4 Of what does Orsino accuse Antonio?

5 Who does Antonio think Cesario is

6 Who threatens to kill Cesario?

7 Who confirms that Olivia has married 'Cesario'?

8 Who beat Sir Toby and Sir Andrew

9 Who returns at the end?

10 Who is married at the end?

Answers

C
1 Fabian 2 Feste 3 when they were in a sea fight 4 of being a pirate 5 Sebastian 6 Orsino 7 the priest 8 Sebastian 9 Sebastian 10 Sir Toby and Maria; Sebastian and Olivia

b
1 very small 2 ship 3 freight 4 Crete 5 shameful past 6 present 7 behaviour tendency 8 natural perspective 9 is suitable 10 love's

a
Sebastian   Viola (Cesario)   Sebastian   Orsino   Cesario
Cesario   Viola   Malvolio   Maria   Sebastian
Orsino   Cesario   Viola
                    Feste

Commentary

Themes

Twelfth Night is a **romantic comedy** (see Literary Terms), an Elizabethan style of play that Shakespeare developed with great success. A romantic comedy usually concerns the love of an idealised couple who, after a series of misadventures and confusions, are finally united. Disguised characters and a far-off setting are also typical features of the romantic comedy. However, although the play is called a 'comedy', its themes are serious, as Shakespeare examines different aspects of human love.

Love

The play's opening lines tell us its major theme, 'If music be the food of love, play on', and some form of love, real or imagined, rules the emotions of all the main and some of the minor characters.

There are five unrequited lovers in the play – Orsino, Sir Andrew and Malvolio all love Olivia; Olivia loves Cesario; Viola loves Orsino

Firstly we are shown the idealised love of Orsino for Olivia whom he loves at a distance and through the messages he sends with Viola (Cesario). He is not dismayed by the fact that Olivia cannot respond; on the contrary, Orsino sees Olivia's decision to mourn her brother's death and live like a nun as proof of her 'sweet perfections' (I.1.39).

Such deluded aspects of love are echoed in the love Olivia feels for Cesario, but here the deception is based on physical appearance. The figure of the deluded lover is made fun of through Malvolio who believes unquestioningly that his beautiful mistress loves him. Both Duke Orsino and Malvolio are in different ways ruled by 'self-love'.

Viola's love for Orsino is, however, selfless. She endures with patience the 'barful strife' of her situation, wooing

Love

another woman for the man she secretly loves, and only able to express her feelings indirectly. Another example of selfless love is seen in the way that Antonio treats Sebastian.

Disguise

'Nothing that is so, is so' (IV.1.8–9)

Women's parts were played by boy actors in Shakespeare's day, so the original Elizabethan audience would have found particular fun in Viola's part: a boy actor dressing up as a woman who, in the play, disguises herself as a man. Viola's disguise, in fact, is a key part of the plot. It allows the audience to know more of the true situation when Olivia and Orsino are on stage, and it is the cause of many of the confusions that make up the story.

Disguises produce confusions of meaning and emotion throughout the play

Many forms of disguise occur in the play. Olivia's pretence at mourning is quickly discarded when she meets Cesario. Orsino's love for Olivia can be seen as an elaborate pretence when it gives way to murderous anger in Act V, before he rapidly transfers his affections to Viola. Feste adopts a disguise to torment Malvolio in Act IV. Sir Toby Belch disguises his real reasons for being friendly with Sir Andrew Aguecheek. And even Malvolio's yellow stockings and cross garters are a kind of pretence.

The play is full of references to these different forms of disguise, to the gap between what appears to be true and what really is true. Viola calls disguise 'a wickedness / Wherein the pregnant enemy does much' (II.2.26–7) when she realises that Olivia has fallen in love with her persona as Cesario. Disguise and self-deception create much frustration and confusion.

Disguised characters were often used in **romantic comedy** (see Literary Terms).

The festive spirit

The importance of pleasure, tolerance and generosity are emphasised in *Twelfth Night*, as you might expect of a play written to be performed during the Christmas season. The 'Twelfth Night' festivities, held on 6 January, were celebrated by Queen Elizabeth and her court with a great banquet followed by an entertainment. The melancholic atmosphere in Olivia's house contrasts with the carefree values of Sir Toby, and when Malvolio is sent to stop the party in Act II scene 3 the conflict between pleasure and Puritanism is brought to a head. 'Dost thou think because thou art virtuous there shall be no more cakes and ale?' (II.3.114–5).

The play celebrates love and pleasure in the present, for human life is short

A theme of enjoyment runs through the play. We are invited to enjoy youth and life quickly, in the present, for it will soon pass. Feste's song (Act II scene 3) expresses his plea: 'What is love? 'Tis not hereafter, / Present mirth hath present laughter: / What's to come is still unsure' (lines 47–50). Both Olivia and Orsino are missing out on life, Olivia because she behaves like a nun, and Orsino because of his deluded love. In his role as commentator on the 'folly' of his superiors, Feste hints that Olivia's sorrow will quickly pass: 'As there is no true cuckold but calamity, so beauty's a flower' (I.5.49–50). He is suggesting that Olivia's mourning is foolish and that she should be giving her young life to love.

Characters

Orsino

Melancholic

In love with love

Eloquent and
poetic

Inconsistent

Passive

Duke Orsino's opening speech in Act I tells us something about his character and mood; he is in love, but this does not bring him happiness, rather a profound melancholy. His speech turns to images of disease and death – 'excess ... surfeiting ... sicken ... die ... dying' – and it is clear that Orsino is not an active lover focused on his beloved. He is preoccupied with the sensation of love itself, feeding his emotions with music and poetry. Orsino has probably seen Olivia only once, and her image has inspired in him a mistaken belief that if she does not love him in return, he will die.

Orsino is an inconsistent character as Feste points out in Act II scene 4, with a mind of 'opal'. He begs for music to reflect his mood, then quickly becomes bored. This changeable nature, however, makes it easy to believe that he can suddenly transfer his affection from Olivia to Viola at the end of the play.

However, he is described by Olivia in Act I scene 5 as 'virtuous ... noble ...', a wealthy, well-educated, polite and handsome man. These are the qualities that make Viola fall in love with him.

Viola

Viola stands between the two extremes of emotion represented by Orsino and Olivia.

When we first meet her in Act I we learn that she is a practical person who makes the best of her situation as a shipwrecked orphan and a woman in a strange land. Her decision to disguise herself as a eunuch shows both courage and resourcefulness.

Viola is intelligent, witty and charming throughout the play, and these qualities enable her to gain Orsino's

Practical
Resourceful
Trusting
Intelligent
Loyal
Honest

special confidence and make Olivia fall in love with her at first sight. Her conversations with Orsino and Olivia show that she is an honest, straightforward character (she deceives others by dressing as a man only so she can survive). She loyally continues to try to win Olivia's love for Orsino, even though she loves him herself. And she treats Olivia with dignity when the countess has confessed her love for her (as Cesario).

Olivia

Virtuous
Melancholic
Self-deceived
Intelligent
Impetuous
Compassionate

Olivia's beauty is the cause of Orsino's poetic love in the first scene.

Her extravagant vow to mourn her brother for seven years shows she is capable of self-deception, as the play subsequently demonstrates when she forgets her vow and falls in love with Cesario.

But Olivia has other, more attractive qualities. She is seen as intelligent and adaptable in her dealings with members of her household. Her response to Malvolio's humiliation also reveals a compassionate nature.

Olivia, however, has a capacity for impetuous feeling. She pursues Cesario relentlessly, with little concern for the dignity that she should show as a countess.

Like Orsino, her feelings at the end are quickly transferred from one object of love to another.

Sir Toby Belch

Carefree
Irresponsible
Witty
Manipulative
Self-interested

Olivia's uncle is a large, earthy and jolly knight who is devoted to pleasures of the flesh, as his name suggests and as his behaviour throughout the play indicates. He is also a witty person, even when he is drunk.

When he is with Sir Andrew, Sir Toby displays a manipulative side to his character. He fools the gullible knight into believing that he could marry Olivia so that he will remain in her house and continue to pay for Sir Toby's drinking. He loves a practical joke, especially when it is ingenious.

Sir Toby can be rather a bully: he makes fun of Sir Andrew and Malvolio. However, when there is a real possibility that Olivia will throw him out of the house, he loses interest in the two tricks, and looks after himself.

Malvolio

Puritanical

Self-important

Humourless

Malvolio is Olivia's steward and an important member of her household. But he is not as important as he would like to be.

Malvolio is always serious and he has absolutely no sense of humour. He believes in dignity, good manners and order.

He is revealed as a hypocrite and a self-centred man, an easy target for the practical jokers.

At the end of the play Malvolio is excluded from the general happiness and good fortune of the other main characters. He still cannot understand why the others want to make a fool of him.

Sir Andrew Aguecheek

A tall, thin and very stupid knight. Sir Toby has invited him to stay in Olivia's house. He is rich, and Sir Toby encourages him to continue wooing the countess so that he will pay for their regular drinking sessions.

Maria

Olivia's servant. She is sharp-witted, practical and inventive; she devises and manages the trick that is played on Malvolio. She eventually marries Sir Toby.

Feste

A clown employed by Countess Olivia. His role in the play is to provide music and witty comment. He moves freely between the households of Olivia and Orsino. He is very good at his job (as Viola recognises in III.1.60) and is paid for his wit on several occasions in the course of the play.

Apart from singing and joking, he also provides comedy when he dresses as 'Sir Topas'. Feste represents the festive spirit of the play, but he can also be rather touchy and cynical.

Sebastian

Viola's twin brother whom she becomes separated from after the shipwreck. He is mistaken for Cesario and marries Olivia.

A handsome, modest, courageous man, Sebastian is rather more emotional than his sister (Viola) and grieves deeply when he thinks she has drowned in the shipwreck.

As the masculine counterpart to Viola (Cesario) he becomes Olivia's 'natural' husband.

Antonio

A sea captain who rescues and befriends Sebastian. He risks his life to follow Sebastian and is arrested by Orsino's officers.

Fabian

A servant of Olivia's. He takes part in the trick against Malvolio and later assists Sir Toby in the trick that is played on Sir Andrew and Cesario.

Language & style

Shakespeare basically uses three styles of writing in his dialogue: **poetic verse**, **blank verse** and **prose** (see Literary Terms).

Poetic verse

Poetic verse uses pairs of rhyming lines (**rhyming couplets** – see Literary Terms) and has a strong rhythm.

'Enough, no more; / 'Tis not so sweet now as it was before. / O spirit of love, how quick and fresh art thou, / That notwithstanding thy capacity / Receiveth as the sea, nought enters there, / Of what validity and pitch soe'er, / But falls into abatement and low price, / Even in a minute! So full of shapes is fancy, / That it alone is high fantastical' (I.1.7–15).

Here Orsino is revealing his inner emotional state in language that is 'poetic' and provides a realistic picture of his emotions. The rhyming words, e.g. 'more ... before' indicate his rather literary, formal expression of love. Note also the **alliterations** (see Literary Terms) in 'capacity ... receiveth ... sea'. The speech uses mostly abstract words, 'spirit of love ... capacity ... validity ... pitch' and the **simile** (see Literary Terms) of the vast sea is Orsino's attempt at philosophy.

Blank verse

Blank verse does not rhyme, except sometimes in the last two lines of a speech to emphasise something. It has the same rhythm or metre of five **iambs** (see Literary Terms) and is close to the stresses of spoken English.

'Well, grant it then, / And tell me, in the modesty of honour, / Why you have given me such clear lights of favour, / Bade me come smiling and cross-garter'd to you, / To put on yellow stockings, and to frown / Upon Sir Toby, and the lighter people' (V.1.333–8).

Prose

Prose is language that does not have a particular rhythm or **metre** (see Literary Terms). It is most often spoken by minor or comic characters in the play. Sometimes it is used to develop the plot or provide important information about a character or an event; for example, when Olivia describes Malvolio in Act I scene 5, she speaks in prose which is memorable for being an accurate picture of his character. About half of the dialogue of *Twelfth Night* is in prose.

Fabian speaks in prose to Sir Andrew: 'She did show favour to the youth in your sight only to exasperate you, to awake your dormouse valour, to put fire in your heart, and brimstone in your liver. You should then have accosted her, and with some excellent jests, fire-new from the mint, you should have banged the youth into dumbness' (III.2.16–22).

Key Stage 3 & Shakespeare

Examinations

Every Year 9 pupil in Britain has to sit Key Stage 3 examinations in English, Mathematics and Science.

There are two English papers:

Paper I: Reading and Writing Test (1 hour 30 minutes plus 15 minutes' reading time)

Paper II: Shakespeare Test (1 hour 15 minutes)

We are not concerned here with Paper I so we shall concentrate upon the Shakespeare requirements.

Three plays are offered each year for study. Each play has two Key Scenes which are the subject of the examination paper. Your teacher will choose which play to study and more than likely the one Key Scene you will have to answer a question on. For the purposes of the examination you will be issued with a booklet containing all six scenes (two from each play), which you can take with you into the examination. There will be a task on each of the scenes and you will have to complete one of these tasks in the time available.

Read the tasks carefully: they give you a clear structure to use in your written response.

A typical question has three parts:

★ A brief description of the scene you have studied

★ Details of the task you have to complete

★ Some prompts to help you arrange your thoughts

I.5: Love is one of the main themes of Twelfth Night. How does Shakespeare approach the theme of love in this scene? Think about:

• what Feste says about marriage

• how Cesario (Viola) talks of Orsino's love

• what we learns about Olivia's attitudes to love

Careful reading

First read the paper calmly and carefully. Take your time over this otherwise you may miss something very obvious – and discover too late that you have been answering the wrong question. It is a good idea to write the task down as the title of your essay on the top of your answer paper, so that it is always there as you are writing and reminds you to keep on the subject.

Using the prompts

Next write notes beside each of the prompts you have been given to help in your response. You could answer the task without bothering about the prompts – but the mark scheme below will make quite plain how important they really are! The prompts are there to help you.

In Key Stage 3, the examiners really are your friends! They know this is the first time you will have sat a public examination on Shakespeare and that you will be nervous, so they are not trying to catch you out!

The mark scheme

You may be surprised to learn that the mark scheme for each question is identical. No matter which play you write about, your performance has to be measured against everyone else's and this would be impossible if there were six different mark schemes.
What the examiner is looking for is the way you have answered the question you attempted.

A typical mark scheme

Achievement in Key Stage 3 is measured in terms of Levels, ranging from 1 up to 7, with 5 considered as the national average.

It is worth looking at the five statements that a mark scheme uses to describe Level 5 achievement:

* Answer selects *some appropriate moments* from the extract, and the significance of *some of these* is clearly explained
* *Some use of quotation*, though the answer may tend to present a general argument rather than a detailed account
* Points made will *generally be quite straightforward* ones
* *Some attempt* to link together points to form a coherent argument
* All of the prompts are referred to, but *one or more may not be covered in sufficient depth*

The italicised portions of the mark schemes are the important parts which the examiner will apply to your answer. If you put all these together, you might end up with this description of your essay:

The candidate knows the scene quite well and has used a few quotations which provide a general answer to the task though some parts are not covered very carefully.

The object of this Note on Twelfth Night is:

* To help you understand the play
* To enable you to answer the questions successfully

Success at Key Stage 3

The key to success is to enjoy the play. This enjoyment comes from hard work. You must first understand precisely what happens in the scene you are studying. Shakespeare's language can be a little complicated but it is English and it all makes sense.

The first step is to read the scene quite quickly and get a rough idea of what happens. Then go through it more slowly getting a general idea of what each speech is about. If you have difficulties with phrases here and there, don't worry, the important thing is to get the gist of what each speech is about.

A good idea as you are studying is to listen to the words being spoken by a professional actor. Follow the scene in your book as the video or audiotape is being played. Or ask your teacher to read the speech out loud for you. When you hear Shakespeare read aloud by someone who understands it, you will discover that your only problems are individual and unfamiliar words.

Now that you have read and understood what is happening in the chosen scene, you must consider what important aspects of the play are revealed in it.

Examiners do not randomly select scenes for special study: they look for those which are important in particular ways. For Key Stage 3, there are four important aspects which apply to a Shakespearean play:

* The way ideas are presented
* The motivation and behaviour of characters
* The way the plot is developed
* The impact the lines make on the audience

The way ideas are presented

There are many different ways of presenting ideas. If we look at *Twelfth Night*, one of the important themes is disguise. One of the main characters spends most of the play disguised as someone of the opposite sex. In other words, she comes to see what life is like for a man. Changing gender like that is quite a common idea in literature: it gives the character a different perspective, but perhaps you might find it unconvincing? How does

Shakespeare make it as convincing as possible? Under what circumstances might you be fooled by someone pretending to be a member of the other sex?

Answer that question and you may understand why Orsino and Olivia behave as they do.

The motivation ˄nd behaviour of characters

It is often said that we are very good at understanding what makes other people tick, but find it harder to understand what motivates us. But the business of what makes people tick is what we are concerned with in understanding characters' motivation and behaviour.

For instance, we can safely assume that Orsino – like many men – enjoys the sensation of being in love, so he looks for relationships that will offer him what he wants. As the play opens he clearly sees possibilities in a love-affair with Olivia and is certain that she must of course be head over heels in love with him. So when she rejects him and says she is going into mourning for seven years for her brother, he doesn't see it as rejection, but as proof of how much love she can give to a man.

The way the plot is developed

Shakespeare is a very accomplished storyteller. We take that for granted. But think for a moment about the art of telling a story. If it was entirely predictable, a story would surely be quite boring. After all, part of the fun of a story is not quite knowing where it is going next or how things will finally turn out.

Look at the opening two scenes of the play. Try and work out for yourself how the events in the second scene may affect the way the story is going to develop as far as Orsino is concerned. By doing this, you are seeing the way the plot develops.

The impact the lines make on the audience

Here you are asked to consider your reaction to what is said on stage. Shakespeare was a great writer: nothing is done accidentally. He uses language in two ways: to reflect the speaker's personality, and to create an impression in the audience's mind.

If you listen to the famous opening line of the play,

If music be the food of love, play on ...

you are first struck by the beauty of the line. It is spoken about love by a man who loves being in love. The play thus starts in a poetic style which is appropriate to a love story. Yet if you look at the sense of the line, you might also wonder if Orsino is being serious: after all, for most people love needs a little more than music if it is to grow! Now you can begin to appreciate the impact that Shakespeare's lines might have upon his audience.

Using quotations

One of the ways in which candidates achieve high grades in an English literature examination is by the use they make of quotations. The important thing to realise is that a quotation can back up the point that you wish to make.

Here are five basic points you must remember:

* Put quotation marks (inverted commas) at the beginning and end of the quotation
* Write the quotation exactly as it appears in the original
* Do not use a quotation that repeats what you have just written

✳ Use the quotation so that it fits into your sentence

✳ Keep the quotation as short as possible

Quotations should be used to develop the line of thought in your essay.

Your comment should not duplicate what is in your quotations. For example:

Viola (in Act II, scene 2 of *Twelfth Night*) tells us that she thinks disguises are wicked, 'Disguise, I see thou art a wickedness'.

It is far more effective to write:

Viola describes disguise as 'a wickedness'.

Always lay out lines as they appear in the original:

Viola answers Orsino's question with a riddle: 'I am all the daughters of my father's house, / And all the brothers too: and yet I know not'.

or:

'I am all the daughters of my father's house,

And all the brothers too: and yet I know not.'

However, the most sophisticated way of using the writer's words is to include them within your own sentence:

Is it really Malvolio's 'self-love' which makes him easy to trick?

Use Shakespeare's words as evidence to support your ideas. Don't just include words from the original to prove you have read it!

Literary terms

alliteration a sequence of repeated sounds in a passage of language

blank verse unrhymed iambic pentameter: a line of five iambs

dramatic irony this occurs when the audience know more about what is happening than some of the characters themselves know

hyperbole a figure of speech that relies on exaggeration

iamb the commonest metrical foot in English verse, a weak stress followed by a strong stress, ti-tum

iambic pentameter a line of five iambic feet. The most common metrical pattern found in English verse

metre this is the pattern of stressed and unstressed syllables in a line of verse

oxymoron a figure of speech in which contrasting terms are brought together: 'The Fortunate Unhappy' (II.5.159)

poetic verse a style of speech in Shakespeare's plays using rhyming couplets and a strong rhythmic pulse to the line

prose any language that is not patterned by the regularity of some kind of metre

pun a play on words: two different meanings are drawn out of a single word, usually for comedy

rhyming couplet a pair of rhymed lines, of any metre e.g. 'O time, thou must untangle this, not I, / It is too hard a knot for me t'untie' (II.2.139–40)

romantic comedy an Elizabethan style of comedy concerning love, difficulties often involving mistaken identities, an escape from the real world into a magical setting, and a happy ending (see also *As You Like It*)

simile a figure of speech in which one thing is said to be like another, always containing the word 'like' or 'as'

soliloquy a dramatic convention which allows a character in a play to speak directly to the audience – as if thinking aloud about motives, feelings and decisions

sub-plot a 'minor' plot in a play or a novel; a story that happens at the same time as the main plot

NOTES

NOTES

GCSE and equivalent levels (£3.50 each)

Maya Angelou
I Know Why the Caged Bird Sings

Jane Austen
Pride and Prejudice

Alan Ayckbourn
Absent Friends

Elizabeth Barrett Browning
Selected Poems

Robert Bolt
A Man for All Seasons

Harold Brighouse
Hobson's Choice

Charlotte Brontë
Jane Eyre

Emily Brontë
Wuthering Heights

Shelagh Delaney
A Taste of Honey

Charles Dickens
David Copperfield

Charles Dickens
Great Expectations

Charles Dickens
Hard Times

Charles Dickens
Oliver Twist

Roddy Doyle
Paddy Clarke Ha Ha Ha

George Eliot
Silas Marner

George Eliot
The Mill on the Floss

William Golding
Lord of the Flies

Oliver Goldsmith
She Stoops To Conquer

Willis Hall
The Long and the Short and the Tall

Thomas Hardy
Far from the Madding Crowd

Thomas Hardy
The Mayor of Casterbridge

Thomas Hardy
Tess of the d'Urbervilles

Thomas Hardy
The Withered Arm and other Wessex Tales

L.P. Hartley
The Go-Between

Seamus Heaney
Selected Poems

Susan Hill
I'm the King of the Castle

Barry Hines
A Kestrel for a Knave

Louise Lawrence
Children of the Dust

Harper Lee
To Kill a Mockingbird

Laurie Lee
Cider with Rosie

Arthur Miller
The Crucible

Arthur Miller
A View from the Bridge

Robert O'Brien
Z for Zachariah

Frank O'Connor
My Oedipus Complex and other stories

George Orwell
Animal Farm

J.B. Priestley
An Inspector Calls

Willy Russell
Educating Rita

Willy Russell
Our Day Out

J.D. Salinger
The Catcher in the Rye

William Shakespeare
Henry IV Part 1

William Shakespeare
Henry V

William Shakespeare
Julius Caesar

William Shakespeare
Macbeth

William Shakespeare
The Merchant of Venice

William Shakespeare
A Midsummer Night's Dream

William Shakespeare
Much Ado About Nothing

William Shakespeare
Romeo and Juliet

William Shakespeare
The Tempest

William Shakespeare
Twelfth Night

George Bernard Shaw
Pygmalion

Mary Shelley
Frankenstein

R.C. Sherriff
Journey's End

Rukshana Smith
Salt on the Snow

John Steinbeck
Of Mice and Men

Robert Louis Stevenson
Dr Jekyll and Mr Hyde

Jonathan Swift
Gulliver's Travels

Robert Swindells
Daz 4 Zoe

Mildred D. Taylor
Roll of Thunder, Hear My Cry

Mark Twain
Huckleberry Finn

James Watson
Talking in Whispers

William Wordsworth
Selected Poems

A Choice of Poets

Mystery Stories of the Nineteenth Century including The Signalman

Nineteenth Century Short Stories

Poetry of the First World War

Six Women Poets